An I Can Read Book®

SNOWSHOE THOMPSON

Nancy Smiler Levinson

PICTURES BY
Joan Sandin

HarperCollins*Publishers*

*To Joanne Rocklin,
my kindred spirit*
—N.S.L.

*For Christopher Horger
and Chris Nordensson,
my models*
—J.S.

CONTENTS

I Can Read Book is a registered trademark
of HarperCollins Publishers.
SNOWSHOE THOMPSON
Text copyright © 1992 by Nancy Smiler Levinson
Illustrations copyright © 1992 by Joan Sandin
Printed in the U.S.A. All rights reserved.
1   2   3   4   5   6   7   8   9   10
First Edition

Library of Congress Cataloging-in-Publication Data
Levinson, Nancy Smiler.
    Snowshoe Thompson / by Nancy Smiler Levinson ; pictures by Joan
Sandin.
    p.   cm. — (An I can read book)
    Summary: One winter John Thompson skis across the Sierra Nevada
and creates a path upon which mail and people may travel, thus earning
his nickname "Snowshoe Thompson."
    ISBN 0-06-023801-1. — ISBN 0-06-023802-X (lib. bdg.)
    1. Thompson, Snowshoe, 1827-1876—Juvenile literature.
2. Pioneers—Sierra Nevada Mountains Region (Calif. and Nev.)—
Biography—Juvenile literature.   3. Postal service—Sierra Nevada
Mountains Region (Calif. and Nev.)—Letter carriers—Biography—
Juvenile literature.   4. Frontier and pioneer life—Sierra Nevada
Mountains Region (Calif. and Nev.)—Juvenile literature.   5. Sierra
Nevada Mountains Region (Calif. and Nev.)—History—Juvenile
literature.   [1. Thompson, Snowshoe, 1827-1876.   2. Postal service—
Letter carriers.   3. Pioneers.   4. Frontier and pioneer life—West
(U.S.)]   I. Sandin, Joan, ill.   II. Title.   III. Series.
F868.S5T485   1992   90-37401
979.4'404'092—dc20   CIP
[B]   AC
[92]

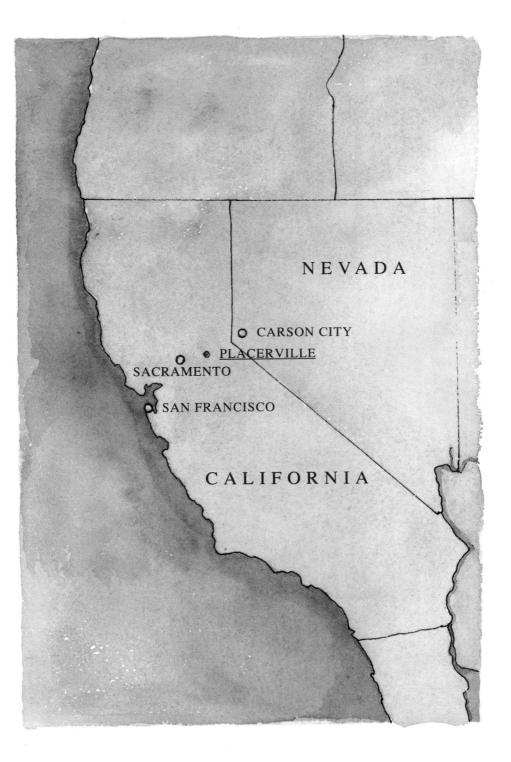

A Letter for Pa

It was a few weeks before Christmas.

Danny O'Riley waited

for the mail coach

at the Placerville Post Office.

7

Danny had a letter

to send to his pa.

It said,

Dear Pa,

You have been gone a long time.

Aunt Nan and I count the days.

I wish you would come home.

Are you still digging for gold

in Nevada?

I do not care

if you strike it rich.

I miss you.

I wish you could come home

for Christmas.

Your son, Danny.

The door opened.

Old Joe, the clerk, came in.

"I have bad news," he said.

"No mail until spring.

The snow is too deep."

Danny blinked back tears

and put his letter in his pocket.

"What good is my letter now?"

he asked Aunt Nan.

"Pa will not know

how much I miss him.

Maybe he will never come back."

"Hush now, lad," said Aunt Nan.

"You will have to wait until spring.

Nothing can get over

the mountains now,

not even the mail."

Just then John Thompson

stepped forward.

He was new in town.

"No mail all winter?"

John asked.

"That's right,"

Old Joe said.

"Many men have tried to cross

the Sierra Nevada mountains,

but few have made it.

The mountains are mighty

dangerous in the snow."

"I can make it," said John.

"How?" asked Danny.

"There is a way," John said.

"Come to my cabin tomorrow,

and you will see."

17

2
Making Skis

John was chopping a log.

Whack! Thwack!

"What are you doing?"

Danny asked.

John looked up

and wiped his brow.

"I am making skis

to deliver the mail,"

he said.

"What are skis?"

asked Danny.

18

"Skis are like snowshoes,"
said John,
"but skis glide fast over the snow.
Everyone in Norway uses them
to go from place to place
in wintertime."
"Will they get you
over the mountains?"
Danny asked.
"Sure," said John.

John swung his axe.

Whack! Thwack! Whack!

He split the log again and again.

"There! We have two long planks

of wood. Now we have

to make the wood

as smooth as glass."

"Can I help?" Danny asked.

"Yes," said John.

"After I shape the planks of wood,

you can help me sand them down."

Scrape! Scrape!

Scratch! Scratch!

Danny's arm felt tired,
but he did not stop.

"You are doing a good job,"

John told Danny.

Danny smiled.

He did not feel so tired anymore.

At last the wood

was as smooth as glass.

"Are the skis done now?"

Danny asked.

"Not yet," said John.

"Now we have to boil the wood."

"Boil the wood?" asked Danny.

"Yes," said John.

"We have to make the tips soft
so we can bend them."
"How long will it take?"
asked Danny.
"Maybe until sundown,"
said John.
Danny watched
the boiling water
bubble over the wood.

"Is the wood soft now?"
Danny asked.

"Yes," said John.

"Now we will wedge

the soft tips of wood

between these two logs.

That will make the tips curve.

Tomorrow the skis will be dry.

I will try them out at sunup."

Danny put his hand in his pocket.

"Soon my letter

will be on the way to Pa,"

he said.

"You can count on me,"

said John.

3

Gliding on Snow

The sun rose over Hangtown Hill.

Danny hurried.

There was John on his skis.

He had a long pole

in one hand.

He was gliding on the snow.

"You are moving fast!" Danny cried.

John came to a stop.

"Now I will try the hill,"

he said.

"Wait," said Danny.

"Let me get Aunt Nan.

She will want to see this."

Everyone came to watch.

37

"Here I go!" John called.

Whoosh! Swish! Whoosh!

"John will hit a tree

and dash his brains out,"

Old Joe said.

Aunt Nan screamed.

"Foolhardy!" another man cried.

"John is not foolhardy!"

said Danny.

"He will deliver the mail.

We can count on him."

4

Over the Mountains

It was a bright, cold morning.

John was ready to leave.

He had a big bag of mail

on his back,

and his skis were strapped

to his boots.

"When will you be back?"

Danny asked.

"I am not sure,"

said John.

"These mountains
are new to me.
But do not worry.
I will be back!"

John set out on his trip.

He skied across meadows

and up and down slopes.

He skied on and on.

Suddenly the sky turned gray

and snow began to fall.

The wind howled.

It blew so hard

that John could barely see.

"The town folks were right,"

John said to himself.

"The Sierra Nevadas are

mighty dangerous in winter."

46

John had a long way to go—
almost ninety miles altogether.
But he did not give up.
He did not turn back.

5

Good News for Danny!

Danny pressed his nose

against the post-office window

and stared at the mountains.

"John has been gone for five days," said Danny.

"Poor John," said Aunt Nan.

"I hope he is still alive."

"Maybe the fellow froze to death," one man said.

"Maybe he was attacked by wolves," said the man's wife.

"John will be back," Danny said.

"I know he will."

Suddenly Old Joe cried,

"Look! There's that fellow

with those crazy snowshoes!"

Danny ran outside.

"I knew you would make it,"

cried Danny.

"I told you

you could count on me,"

said John.

He opened the mailbag

and pulled out a letter.

"Here, Danny, this is for you."

Danny tore open the letter.

He read:

Dear Danny,

I was very happy

to get your letter.

I miss you too.

I will be home for Christmas.

I cannot wait to see you.

Love from your pa.

"How will Pa get here?"
Danny asked John.

"On skis!" said John.

"We are going to make

a pair of skis

for your pa."

"Pa is coming home on skis,"
cried Danny.

"Pa will be home for Christmas!"

AUTHOR'S NOTE

This tale is based on the true story of John Thompson. Born in Norway, he went to Placerville, California, in the early 1850s to seek his fortune in the gold rush. John was one of many Scandinavian immigrants who introduced skis to America.

During the winter, when the Sierra Nevada cut off northern California from the rest of the country, John braved the long and treacherous journey over the mountains on skis to deliver bags of mail, which often weighed as much as 100 pounds. On his five-day journey he had only dried beef and biscuits to eat, the snow to quench his thirst, and caves for shelter at night. Even then, he often rescued many lost and half-frozen men along the way.

Local folks took to calling him Snowshoe Thompson. Although he never struck it rich digging for gold, he managed to become a legend of the gold rush days.